Smithsonian

LITTLE EXPLORER

APATOSAURUS

by Sally Lee

CAPSTONE PRESS
a capstone imprint

Little Explorer is published by Capstone Press,
1710 Roe Crest Drive, North Mankato, Minnesota 56003
www.capstoneyoungreaders.com

The name of the Smithsonian Institution and the sunburst
logo are registered trademarks of the Smithsonian Institution.
For more information, please visit www.si.edu.

Library of Congress Cataloging-in-Publication Data

Lee, Sally, 1943– author.
Apatosaurus / by Sally Lee.
pages cm. — (Smithsonian Little explorer. Little paleontologist)
Summary: "Introduces young readers to Apatosaurus, including
physical characteristics, habitat, behavior, diet, and fossil
discovery"— Provided by publisher.
Audience: Ages 4–7
Audience: K to grade 3.
Includes index.
ISBN 978-1-4914-2128-4 (library binding)
ISBN 978-1-4914-2375-2 (paperback)
ISBN 978-1-4914-2379-0 (paper over board)
ISBN 978-1-4914-2383-7 (eBook PDF)
1. Apatosaurus—Juvenile literature.
2. Paleontology—Jurassic—Juvenile
literature. 3. Dinosaurs—Juvenile literature.
I. Title.
QE862.S3L438 2015
567.913'8—dc23   2014021792

Editorial Credits

Michelle Hasselius, editor; Heidi Thompson,
designer; Wanda Winch, media researcher;
Tori Abraham, production specialist

Our very special thanks to Mike Brett-Surman, PhD, Museum
Specialist for Fossil Dinosaurs, Reptiles, Amphibians, and
Fish at the National Museum of Natural History, Smithsonian
Institution, for his curatorial review. Capstone would also
like to thank Kealy Wilson, Product Development Manager,
and the following at Smithsonian Enterprises: Ellen Nanney,
Licensing Manager; Brigid Ferraro, Vice President, Education
and Consumer Products; Carol LeBlanc, Senior Vice President,
Education and Consumer Products.

Image Credits

Capstone: Steve Weston, 29 (bottom); Dr. Jack
Share, 25 (top right); Getty Images: Chicago
Field Museum Library, 27 (t), Chicago Field
Museum Library/Charles Carpenter, 26, De
Agostini, 9 (b), 22, The Print Collector, 28–29;
iStockphoto: milehightraveler, 24–25; Jon
Hughes, cover, 1–9, 11, 12–18, 20–21; Peabody
Museum of Natural History, Yale University,
24 (m); Richard A. Paselk, 19; Sauropod
embryo model by William Monteleon,
Photo courtesy of StoneCompany.com, 23;
Science Source: Francois Gohier, 10, Richard
Bizley, 30–31; Shutterstock: BACO, 4 (bus),
Catmando, 17 (ml), 21 (tr), dkvektor, 17 (mr),
DM7, 17 (bl), Four Oaks, 7 (t), Linda Bucklin,
17 (tr), Petr Masek, 11 (tl), reallyround, 5
(br), Steffen Foerster, 5 (bl), T4W4, 4 (folder),
Viktorya170377, 17 (tl, tm, br); Sinclair Oil
Company, 27 (b); Visuals Unlimited: Scott
Berner, 15 (br)

Printed in the United States of America in
Stevens Point, Wisconsin.
092014   008479WZS15

TABLE OF CONTENTS

name: Apatosaurus

how to say it: uh-pat-oh-SAW-rus

when it lived: late Jurassic Period,
Mesozoic Era

what it ate: plants

size: up to 100 feet
(30.5 meters) long
15 feet (4.6 m) tall from
the ground to the hips
weighed 33 to 38 tons
(30 to 34.5 metric tons)

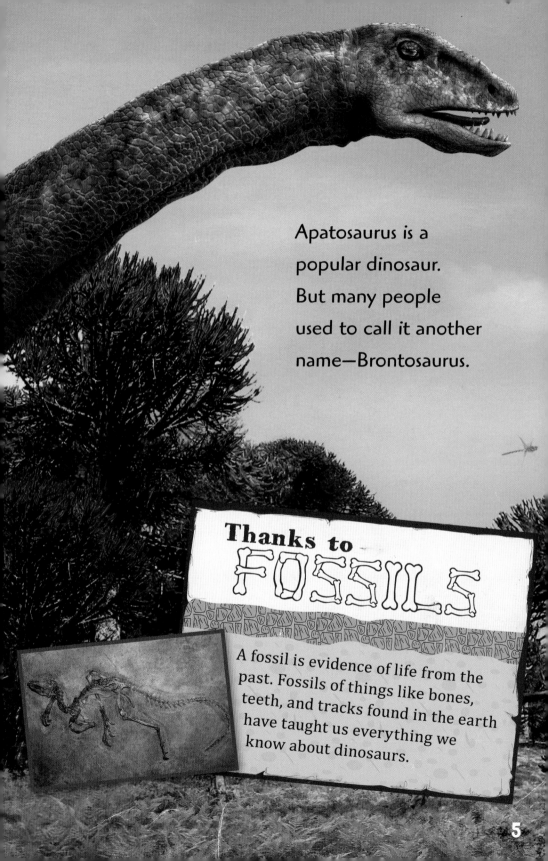

Apatosaurus is a popular dinosaur. But many people used to call it another name—Brontosaurus.

Thanks to FOSSILS

A fossil is evidence of life from the past. Fossils of things like bones, teeth, and tracks found in the earth have taught us everything we know about dinosaurs.

PREHISTORIC GIANT

nostrils on top of head

long neck

small head with a tiny brain

one large claw on each front foot

Apatosaurus was a huge dinosaur. It was as long as two city buses. It weighed as much as five elephants.

Apatosaurus was part of a group of dinosaurs called sauropods. The four-legged dinosaurs had long necks and tails.

whiplike tail

thick legs

five toes on each foot

A TAIL FOR A WEAPON

Apatosaurus's tail was about 50 feet (15 m) long. That's more than half the length of its body. The dinosaur's tail was as thick as a trash can near its body. It ended in a skinny whip.

Apatosaurus used its whipping tail to protect itself. One powerful strike could hurt or knock over a predator.

Allosaurus and
Apatosaurus

Allosaurus was Apatosaurus's main
predator. But Apatosaurus was up
to 10 times bigger than Allosaurus.

HEAVY STEPS

Apatosaurus walked on four thick legs.
Its back legs were longer than its front legs.

Apatosaurus had a large claw on each of
its front feet. Apatosaurus's feet had five
toes. Thick padding on the bottom of its
feet helped soften its heavy footsteps.

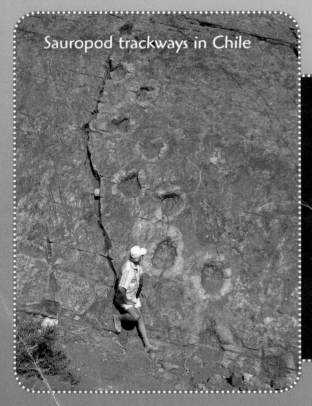

Sauropod trackways in Chile

Over time the mud
dinosaurs walked on
turned to stone. Their
footprints can still
be seen in the stone
millions of years later.
These fossil footprints
are called trackways.
They give scientists
clues about where
dinosaurs lived and
how they moved.

Siberian tiger

Heavy animals like tigers also have padded feet.

LONG NECK

Apatosaurus had a neck that was about 40 feet (12 m) long. A long neck let the dinosaur poke its head into places where its giant body couldn't fit. It could reach food without moving its body. Apatosaurus could stand on dry ground and eat plants growing in muddy swamps.

Apatosaurus couldn't lift its head straight up. It swept its head from side to side.

TINY HEAD

Apatosaurus had a small head. It was about 2 feet (0.6 m) long.

The dinosaur had peglike teeth in the front of its mouth. Apatosaurus used its teeth to strip off leaves and gather plants. There were no teeth in the back of its mouth.

The dinosaur's brain was smaller than many other dinosaurs alive at that time.

Apatosaurus's nostrils were on top of its head. Scientists once thought this meant it lived in water. Now scientists know more about how Apatosaurus lived. The dinosaur's trackways show that it only lived on land.

dinosaur trackways on land

JURASSIC HOME

Apatosaurus lived in what is now the western United States. It made its home in the states of Colorado, Oklahoma, Utah, Montana, and Wyoming.

This area had warm and dry seasons during the late Jurassic Period. Plants and trees grew easily.

The largest land animals of all time first appeared during the Jurassic Period.

Other Jurassic Animals

Allosaurus

Brachiosaurus

Camarasaurus

Camptosaurus

Diplodocus

Ceratosaurus

Stegosaurus

The Jurassic Period lasted from 200 million to 145 million years ago.

DINOSAUR ERA

TRIASSIC	JURASSIC	CRETACEOUS

252   200   145   66   present

millions of years ago

BIG EATER

Some scientists think Apatosaurus ate up to 1 ton (0.9 metric ton) of food each day.

Apatosaurus was an herbivore. This means it ate only plants.

The dinosaur ate conifers, cycads, and ginkgo trees. It also ate low-growing plants like mosses and ferns.

gastroliths

Apatosaurus swallowed its food whole. It also swallowed stones called gastroliths. The stones helped grind up the tough plants in the dinosaur's stomach.

LIVING ALONE

Apatosaurus may have lived alone instead of in herds. No Apatosaurus fossils have ever been found in groups.

Apatosaurus spent most of its day eating. Because of its huge size, Apatosaurus had to keep moving to find more food.

The dinosaur's size kept most predators away.

EGGS AND BABIES

Apatosaurus hatched from an egg smaller than a soccer ball. A female Apatosaurus laid her eggs in a line while walking. Females did not take care of their eggs or babies. Scientists decided this because footprints do not show young Apatosauruses traveling with adults.

Oviraptor ate the eggs of other dinosaurs.

Most Apatosaurus babies never became adults. They were killed by predators.

a model of a sauropod egg

Apatosaurus babies were less than 2 feet (0.6 m) long. They weighed about 22 pounds (10 kilograms).

MONSTROUS BONES

Geologist Arthur Lakes was studying rocks near the Morrison Formation in Colorado in 1877. He found huge bones. Lakes sent some of the bones to paleontologist Othniel Marsh.

Arthur Lakes

They were "*so monstrous ... so utterly beyond anything I had ever read or conceived possible ... *"—from the journal of Arthur Lakes

Thousands of fossils from Jurassic dinosaurs have been found in the Morrison Formation. This area of layered rock covers much of the western United States.

Morrison Formation

MIXED-UP NAMES

Marsh named the bones Lakes found "Apatosaurus" in 1877. Two years later Marsh named a larger set of bones "Brontosaurus."

Elmer Riggs (right) and his assistant studied fossils in his lab.

But Marsh goofed. Paleontologist Elmer Riggs studied Lakes' bones again in 1903. He found the fossils thought to be a young Brontosaurus were really from Apatosaurus. This means the same dinosaur had two different names. The name "Apatosaurus" was used first, so it became the dinosaur's official name.

Elmer Riggs with a Menodus skull

This dinosaur is used as a symbol for Sinclair Oil Corporation.

Brontosaurus was popular in books and cartoons such as *The Flintstones*. Most people didn't want the dinosaur's name to be changed. It took nearly 80 years for the name "Apatosaurus" to be accepted.

WRONG HEAD

The first Apatosaurus fossil didn't have a head. A skull found nearby looked too small to belong to such a large dinosaur. Casts of larger skulls were put on Apatosaurus models in museums. But they were Camarasaurus skulls. For years Apatosaurus models had the wrong heads.

photo of an Apatosaurus skeleton with a Camarasaurus head

Two dinosaur experts thought Apatosaurus had a small head like Diplodocus. They found the right skull in a museum basement. Apatosaurus models have had the right heads since 1979.

Camarasaurus

Camarasaurus was a sauropod that lived during the late Jurassic Period. It was smaller than Apatosaurus. But it had a bigger head.

GLOSSARY

cast—an object made by pouring liquid into a mold and letting it harden

conifer—a tree with cones and narrow leaves called needles

cycad—a plant shaped like a tall pineapple, with a feathery crown of palmlike leaves

fern—a plant with finely divided leaves known as fronds; ferns are common in damp woods and on mountains

fossil—evidence of life from the geologic past

gastrolith—stomach stones used for grinding up food

geologist—a scientist who studies rocks to learn how the earth has changed over time

ginkgo—a tree with green, fan-shaped leaves

Jurassic Period—the second period of the Mesozoic Era; when birds first appeared

Mesozoic Era—the age of dinosaurs, which includes the Triassic, Jurassic, and Cretaceous periods; when the first birds, mammals, and flowers appeared

nostrils—openings in the nose used to breathe and smell

paleontologist—a scientist who studies fossils

predator—an animal that hunts other animals for food

trackway—a set of footprints from long ago found in rocks

CRITICAL THINKING USING THE COMMON CORE

Allosaurus was Apatosaurus's main predator. Describe two ways Apatosaurus could protect itself against predators such as Allosaurus. (Key Ideas and Details)

Apatosaurus swallowed gastroliths with its food. What are gastroliths? (Craft and Structure)

Apatosaurus was called Brontosaurus for many years. Describe in your own words why Apatosaurus had two different names. (Integration of Knowledge and Ideas)

READ MORE

Mara, Wil. *Apatosaurus.* Rookie Read-About Dinosaurs. New York: Children's Press, 2012.

Matthews, Rupert. *World's Dumbest Dinosaurs.* Extreme Dinosaurs. Chicago: Heinemann Library, 2012.

Raatma, Lucia. *Apatosaurus.* Dinosaurs. Ann Arbor, Mich.: Cherry Lake Pub., 2013.

INTERNET SITES

FactHound offers a safe, fun way to find Internet sites related to this book. All of the sites on FactHound have been researched by our staff.

Here's all you do:

Visit *www.facthound.com*

Type in this code: 9781491421284

INDEX